EYEWITNESS
WORLD WAR I

Penguin
Random
House

Project editor Patricia Moss
Art editors Julia Harris, Rebecca Painter
Senior editor Monica Byles
Senior art editors Jane Tetzlaff, Clare Shedden
Category publisher Jayne Parsons
Managing art editor Jacquie Gulliver
Senior production controller Kate Oliver
Picture research Sean Hunter
DTP designers Justine Eaton, Matthew Ibbotson

RELAUNCH EDITION (DK UK)
Editor Ashwin Khurana
Senior designers Rachael Grady, Spencer Holbrook
Managing editor Gareth Jones
Managing art editor Philip Letsu
Publisher Andrew Macintyre
Producer (pre-production) Adam Stoneham
Senior producer Charlotte Cade
Jacket editor Fleur Star
Publishing director Jonathan Metcalf
Associate publishing director Liz Wheeler
Art director Phil Ormerod

Special sales and custom publishing manager
Michelle Baxter

RELAUNCH EDITION (DK INDIA)
Senior editor Neha Gupta
Art editor Deep Shikha Walia
Senior DTP designer Harish Aggarwal
DTP designers Anita Yadav, Pawan Kumar
Managing editor Alka Thakur Hazarika
Managing art editor Romi Chakraborty
CTS manager Balwant Singh
Jacket editorial manager Saloni Talwar
Jacket designer Dhirendra Singh

This Eyewitness ® Guide has been conceived by
Dorling Kindersley Limited and Editions Gallimard

This abridged edition published in 2021
Revised edition published in 2014
First published in Great Britain in 2001 by
Dorling Kindersley Limited,
DK, One Embassy Gardens, 8 Viaduct Gardens, London, SW11 7BW

CONTENTS

A fatal shot

The assassins
Gavrilo Princip, above right, fired the fatal shot that sparked the Great War.

On 28 June 1914, the heir to the Austro-Hungarian throne, Archduke Franz Ferdinand, was shot dead in Sarajevo, Bosnia. As Bosnia was claimed by neighbouring Serbia, Austria-Hungary blamed Serbia for the assassination, and on 28 July declared war. Germany supported Austria-Hungary, Russia supported Serbia, and France supported Russia. When Germany invaded neutral Belgium on its way to France, Britain declared war on Germany. The Great War had begun.

Mobilize!
In July 1914, military notices across Europe told citizens that their country was being mobilized (prepared) for war, and that all regular and reserve troops should report for duty.

Germany rejoices
Germany mobilized on 1 August, declaring war against Russia that evening and against France on 3 August. Many civilians rushed to join the army in support of Kaiser and country.

The Austro-Hungarian army
The Austro-Hungarian empire had three armies – Austrian, Hungarian, and the "Common Army". Ten main languages were spoken, leading to frequent communication difficulties.

Austro-Hungarian *Reiter* (Trooper) of the 8th Uhlan (Lancer) Regiment

One day in Sarajevo
Believing that Bosnia should be part of Serbia, six assassins ambushed Archduke Ferdinand on route to the Austrian governor's residence in Sarajevo. One threw a bomb at Ferdinand's car, but it bounced off and exploded minutes later. When Ferdinand and his wife went to visit the injured officers in hospital, Gavrilo Princip mounted the royal car and shot the couple.

Bomb bounced off canopy and landed under following car

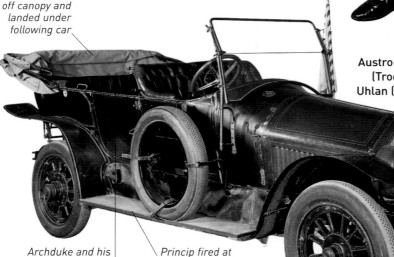

Archduke and his wife Sophie sat in the back of the open-top car

Princip fired at close range from the running board

28 June Archduke Franz Ferdinand is assassinated
5 July Germany gives its ally, Austria-Hungary, total support

23 July Austria issues an ultimatum to Serbia that threatens Serbian independence

25 July Serbia agrees to most of the demands
28 July Austria-Hungary ignores Serbia's terms and declares war

30 July Russia mobilizes in support of its ally, Serbia
1 August Germany mobilizes against Russia and declares

Bekanntmachung.
Mobilmachung befohlen.
Erster Mobilmachungstag, der 2. August

Vorstehender Allerhöchster Befehl wird hierdurch öffentlich bekannt gemacht.

Berlin, den 1. August 1914.

Der Oberbürgermeister
Wermuth.

ARMÉE DE TERRE ET ARMÉE DE MER

ORDRE
DE MOBILISATION GÉNÉRALE

Par décret du Président de la République, la mobilisation des armées de terre et de mer est ordonnée, ainsi que la réquisition des animaux, voitures et harnais nécessaires au complément de ces armées.

Le premier jour de la mobilisation est le Dimanche deux Août 1914

Tout Français soumis aux obligations militaires doit, sous peine d'être puni avec toute rigueur des lois obéir aux prescriptions du FASCICULE DE MOBILISATION (pages coloriées placées dans son livret).

Sont visés par le présent ordre TOUS LES HOMMES non présents sous les Drapeaux et appartenant:

1° à l'ARMÉE DE TERRE y compris les TROUPES COLONIALES et les hommes des SERVICES AUXILIAIRES;

2° à l'ARMÉE DE MER y compris les INSCRITS MARITIMES et les ARMÉES de la MARINE.

German (above) and French (right) mobilization posters

Vive La France
The French army mobilized on 1 August. For many Frenchmen, the war was a chance to seek revenge for the German defeat of France in 1870–71.

All aboard!
The German troops on this westbound train believed that the offensive against France would soon take them to Paris. French troops felt the same about Berlin.

"The lamps are going out all over Europe."

*SIR EDWARD GREY
BRITISH FOREIGN SECRETARY, 1914*

war; France mobilizes in support of its ally, Russia; Germany signs a treaty with Ottoman Turkey; Italy declares its neutrality

2 August Germany invades Luxemburg
3 August Germany declares war on France

4 August Germany invades Belgium on route to France; Britain enters the war to safeguard Belgian neutrality

6 August Austria-Hungary declares war on Russia
12 August France and Britain declare war on Austria-Hungary

War in the west

Christmas treat
The City of London Territorial Association sent each of its soldiers a tinned plum pudding for Christmas in 1914.

By 1905, fearing war on two fronts, Germany's Field Marshal Count Alfred von Schlieffen had developed a plan to knock France swiftly out of any war before turning against Russia. In August 1914, the plan went into operation. German troops crossed the Belgian border on 4 August, and by the end of the month, invaded northern France. At the Battle of the Marne on 5 September, the German advance was held and pushed back. By Christmas 1914, the two sides faced stalemate on the Western Front, along a line from the Belgian coast in the north to the Swiss border in the south.

In retreat
Unable to block the German army, Belgian soldiers with dog-drawn machine guns withdraw to Antwerp.

In the field
The British Expeditionary Force (B.E.F.) had arrived in France by 22 August 1914. Its cavalry division included members of the Royal Horse Artillery, whose L Battery fired this 13-pounder quick-firing Mark I gun against the German 4th Cavalry Division at the Battle of Néry on 1 September.

Steel helmet

Shaft to attach gun to horses that pull the gun along

Soldiers wore puttees, long strips of cloth wrapped around their legs

Third gunner fires the gun on command

First gunner hands shell to second gunner on command

Second gunner loads the shell

The Christmas truce

On Christmas Eve 1914, soldiers on both sides of the Western Front sang carols to each other. The next day, troops along two-thirds of the front observed a truce. All firing stopped, and church services were held. A few soldiers crossed into no-man's-land to talk to their enemy and exchange cigarettes and other gifts. South of Ypres, Belgium, the two sides even played a game of football. One year later, however, sentries on both sides were ordered to shoot anyone attempting a repeat performance.

British soldier shooting at enemy with a note saying "Christmas Eve – Get 'em!"

British and German soldiers greeting each other on Christmas Day

German trench

Eyewitness

Captain E.R.P. Berryman wrote a letter home describing the truce. This cartoon illustrates the absurdity of his situation – shooting the enemy one day and greeting them as friends the next.

Rope wrapped around recoil mechanism

Fires 5.6-kg (12.5-lb) shells a distance of 5,395 m (17,700 ft)

Heading for the front

By early September, German troops were only 40 km (25 miles) east of Paris. The city's military governor used 600 taxis to take 6,000 men to reinforce the front line.

Fighting men

The outbreak of war in August 1914 changed the lives of millions. Regular soldiers, older reservists, eager recruits, and unwilling conscripts were all caught up in the war. Some were experienced soldiers, but many had barely held a rifle before. Britain and France also drew heavily on armies recruited from their empires.

France

Hat flaps could be pulled down to keep out the cold

Winter jerkin made of goat- or sheepskin

Ammunition pouch

Grand Duke Nicholas

In 1914, the Russian army was led by the Tsar's uncle, Grand Duke Nicholas. As commander-in-chief, he dealt with the overall strategy of the war, and his generals directed the battles. The other warring countries had similar chains of command.

Woollen puttees wrapped around shins

The British army

At the start of war, the British army contained just 247,432 regulars and 218,280 reservists. They wore a khaki uniform consisting of a single-breasted tunic, trousers, puttees or leggings worn to protect the shins, and ankleboots.

British soldier

Lee Enfield rifle No. 1 MkIII

Thick boots to protect feet

Russia

Empire troops

Britain and France drew on their colonies in Africa, Asia, the Pacific, and the Caribbean for large numbers of recruits. The British dominions of Australia, New Zealand, Canada, and South Africa also sent their armies to take part in the conflict. Many of these men had never left home before. The Annamites (Indo-Chinese) above, from French Indo-China, were stationed at Salonika, Greece, in 1916.

Eastern allies

In Eastern Europe, Germany faced the vast Russian army, as well as smaller armies from Serbia and Montenegro. In the Far East, German colonies in China and the Pacific Ocean were invaded by Japan.

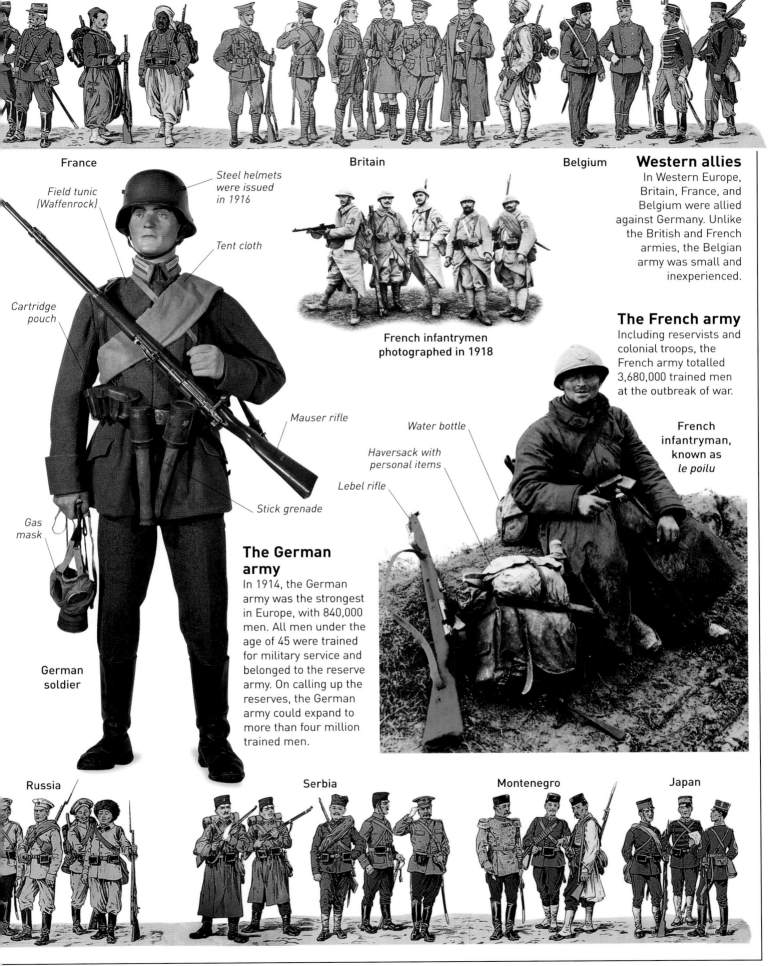

France

Steel helmets were issued in 1916

Field tunic (Waffenrock)

Tent cloth

Cartridge pouch

Mauser rifle

Stick grenade

Gas mask

German soldier

The German army

In 1914, the German army was the strongest in Europe, with 840,000 men. All men under the age of 45 were trained for military service and belonged to the reserve army. On calling up the reserves, the German army could expand to more than four million trained men.

Britain

Belgium

French infantrymen photographed in 1918

Western allies

In Western Europe, Britain, France, and Belgium were allied against Germany. Unlike the British and French armies, the Belgian army was small and inexperienced.

The French army

Including reservists and colonial troops, the French army totalled 3,680,000 trained men at the outbreak of war.

Water bottle

Haversack with personal items

Lebel rifle

French infantryman, known as *le poilu*

Russia

Serbia

Montenegro

Japan

Joining up

At the outbreak of war, unlike Europe's large armies of conscripts, Britain had only a small army made up of volunteers. On 6 August 1914, the Secretary of War, Lord Kitchener, asked for 100,000 new recruits. Whole streets and villages of patriotic men queued to enlist.

War leader
Britain's prime minister in 1914 Herbert Asquith, was known as "the last of the Romans".

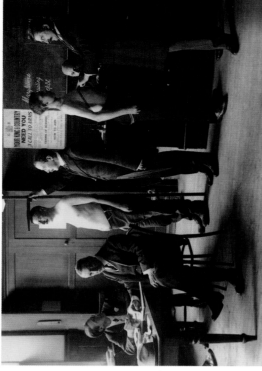

The test
Every British recruit had a medical test to make sure he was fit to fight. Many failed the test, because of poor eyesight or ill health. Others were refused because they were under 19, although many lied about their age.

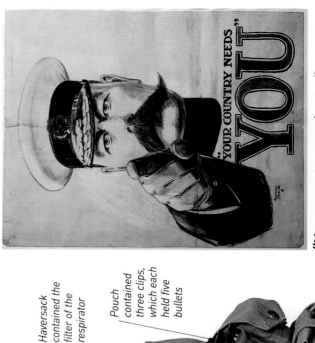

"Your country needs you"
A portrait of Lord Kitchener was used as a recruiting poster in 1914. Some 2,446,719 men had enlisted by1916, but more were needed.

Small box respirator gas mask

Haversack contained the filter of the respirator

Pouch contained three clips, which each held five bullets

Two sets of five ammunition pouches on belt

Queue here for king and country
At the outbreak of war, men from the same area or industry joined Pals battalions, so they could fight together. By mid-September, half a million men had volunteered.

The basic kit

A British soldier carried enough basic equipment to fight and to survive in the trenches: his rifle and bayonet, ammunition, and an entrenching tool to dig a shallow hole to take cover in. By 1917, he also carried a respirator in case of gas attacks. His survival kit included cutlery, a washing kit, and spare clothes. Going into battle, he put the most needed items into a smaller haversack.

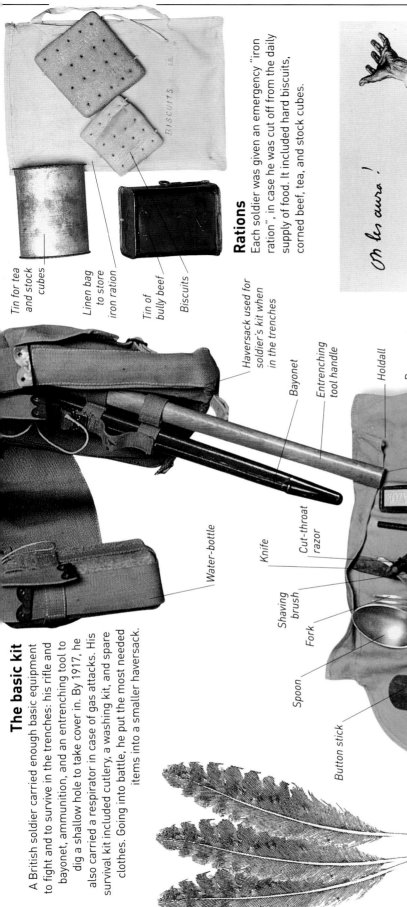

Tin for tea and stock cubes

Linen bag to store iron ration

Tin of bully beef

Biscuits

Haversack used for soldier's kit when in the trenches

Bayonet

Entrenching tool handle

Water-bottle

Knife

Cut-throat razor

Shaving brush

Fork

Spoon

Button stick

Holdall

Razor case

Boot laces

Soldier's small kit

Rations

Each soldier was given an emergency "iron ration", in case he was cut off from the daily supply of food. It included hard biscuits, corned beef, tea, and stock cubes.

2ᴱ EMPRUNT DE LA DÉFENSE NATIONALE *Sousvies*

On les aura !

Paying for the troops

The cost of raising and supplying armies meant each country had to raise taxes. Banks and private investors were asked to lend money to their government in the form of war loans. This French poster drums up support with the words *"On les aura!"* ("We'll get them!").

Empire troops

When war was declared, thousands of men volunteered from across the British Empire. New recruits augmented existing regiments, such as these Bengal Lancers. Indian troops served with distinction, far from home.

Conscientious objectors

Some people who refused to join up were given white feathers as a sign of cowardice. Certain religious groups objected to the war because they believed it was wrong to kill, and some Socialists objected to fighting fellow workers. Both groups were known as conscientious objectors. Some objectors served in non-combatant units, such as medical services.

Stalemate

At the outbreak of war, both sides on the Western Front were equipped with powerful, long-range artillery weapons and rapid-fire machine guns. These weapons made it dangerous for soldiers to fight in unprotected, open ground. So they dug defensive trenches, and found themselves trapped in a static fight.

— Front line of trenches

Blade cover

The front line
By December 1914, a network of trenches ran along the Western Front from the Belgian coast in the north down through eastern France to the Swiss border, 645 km (400 miles) in the south.

The first trenches
Early trenches were just deep furrows, providing minimal cover from enemy fire. Troops from the 2nd Scots Guards dug this trench near Ypres, Belgium, in October 1914.

Entrenching tools
Each soldier carried an entrenching tool. He used it to dig a scrape – a shallow trench – if he was caught out in the open by enemy fire. He could also use it to repair a trench damaged by an enemy artillery bombardment.

American M1910 entrenching tool

DEATH VALLEY

Signposts
Each trench was signposted, often with its nickname, to avoid soldiers losing their way.

Positioning the trench
The Gemans usually built trenches where they could best observe and fire at the enemy while remaining concealed. The British and French preferred to capture as much ground as possible before digging their trenches.

Boarded up

By summer 1915, many German trenches were reinforced with wooden walls to prevent them from collapsing onto the troops and burying them alive. They were also dug very deep to help protect the men from artillery bombardments.

Home sweet home?

The Germans constructed the most elaborate trenches, regarding them as the new German border. Many trenches had shuttered windows and even doormats to wipe muddy boots on!

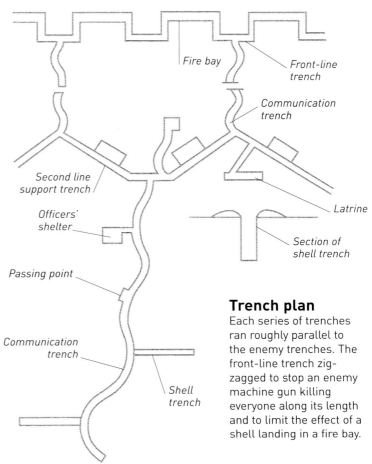

Fire bay

Front-line trench

Communication trench

Second line support trench

Officers' shelter

Latrine

Section of shell trench

Passing point

Communication trench

Shell trench

Trench plan

Each series of trenches ran roughly parallel to the enemy trenches. The front-line trench zigzagged to stop an enemy machine gun killing everyone along its length and to limit the effect of a shell landing in a fire bay.

Coping with the mud

Rain, snow, and natural seepage soon filled trenches with water. Wooden slats, known as duckboards, were laid on the ground to keep soldiers' feet reasonably dry, but it was always muddy.

Bombardment

Sight saver
A chain-mail visor on British helmets made it hard to see and was soon removed.

Beware!
Soldiers at the front needed constant reminders to keep their heads down.

Artillery dominated the battlefields of World War I. A bombardment could destroy enemy trenches, knock out artillery batteries and communication lines, and help break up an infantry attack. As defences strengthened, artillery bombardments became longer and more intense.

Helmet

German armour
In 1916, the German army replaced its spiked *Pickelhaube* helmet with a rounded, steel helmet and issued body armour to machine gunners.

Visor

Breastplate

Articulated plates to cover lower body

Hiding the gun
Light field artillery was pulled by horses, while heavier guns, such as howitzers, were moved by tractors. Once in place, artillery pieces were camouflaged.

British 20-cm (8-in) Mark V howitzer

Shell power
A huge number of shells was needed to maintain a constant artillery barrage. In mid-1917, the British used a million shells a day.

Loading a howitzer

Large pieces of artillery required a team of experienced gunners to load and fire them. This British 38-cm (15-in) howitzer was used on the Menin Road near Ypres in October 1917. Its huge, heavy shell is being winched into position.

Explosion!

In this dramatic picture, a British tank has just been hit by a high-explosive shell. To its right, another tank breaks through the barbed wire. It was unusual for moving targets such as tanks to be hit. Most artillery fire was used to soften up the enemy lines before an attack.

British 5.9-kg (13-lb) high-explosive shell

French 75-mm (2.9-in) shrapnel shell

British 11.4-cm (4.5-in) high-explosive shell

German 15-cm (5.9-in) shrapnel shell

Artillery shells

High-explosive shells exploded on impact. Anti-personnel shrapnel shells exploded in flight, designed to kill or maim.

Over the top

Once the artillery bombardment had pounded the enemy's defences, the infantry climbed out of their trenches and advanced towards enemy lines. But artillery bombardments rarely knocked out every enemy defence, and gaps were filled by highly mobile machine-gunners. A soldier armed with only a rifle and bayonet and laden with heavy equipment was an easy target.

Leaving the trench
The most frightening moment for a soldier was climbing out of his trench and into no-man's-land.

Steel water jacket to cool gun barrel

German MG '08 Maxim machine gun

Disc is part of the flash hider assembly, making the gun harder to spot

Trench mounting

British 7.7-mm (0.303-in) Maxim Mark 3 medium machine gun

Water-cooled barrel

Quick firing
Machine guns fired up to 600 bullets a minute. Ammunition was fitted into a belt, or in a tray fed into the gun automatically.

In action
This German machine-gun crew protects the flank (side) of advancing infantry. The manoeuvrability, reliability, and firepower of machine guns made them effective weapons and difficult for the enemy to destroy.

Tripod mounting

Futile attack

The Battle of the Somme in France lasted from 1 July 1916 until 18 November, when snow and rain brought the attack to a muddy halt. The Allies took about 125 sq km (48 sq miles) of land, but failed to break through the German lines north of the River Somme.

> *"The sunken road... (was)... filled with pieces of uniform, weapons, and dead bodies."*

LIEUTENANT ERNST JUNGER, GERMAN SOLDIER, THE SOMME, 1916

First day on the Somme

The British began a six-day artillery bombardment on 24 June, but the Germans retreated into deep bunkers and were largely unharmed. As the British infantry advanced at 7.30 am on 1 July, German machine gunners opened fire. On that first day alone, they killed or injured two British soldiers along each metre (three feet) of the 25-km (16-mile) front.

Tending the wounded
The cramped conditions in a muddy trench can be seen in this image of an army medical officer tending a wounded soldier at Thiepval near the Somme in September 1916.

Soldiers of the 103rd (Tyneside Irish) Brigade attack La Boisselle on the first day of the Somme

Casualty

An estimated 21 million soldiers were wounded in the war. Caring for casualties was a major military operation. They were first treated in the trenches, then moved to casualty clearing stations behind the front line for proper medical attention, then on to base hospitals still further from the front. Soldiers with severe injuries went home to recover in hospitals.

Lucky man
When a splinter from a shell pierced his helmet, this soldier escaped with only a minor head wound. Many received severe injuries that stayed with them for life.

Inventory listing contents and where to find them in the pouch

Bottles of liquid antiseptics and painkillers

The German kit
German medical orderlies carried two first-aid pouches on their belts. One contained basic antiseptics and painkillers, while the other contained dressings and triangular bandages.

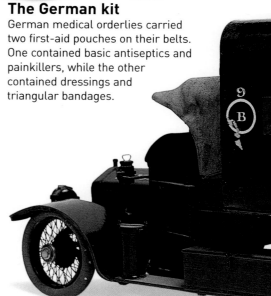

Trench aid
Injured soldiers had their wounds dressed by medical orderlies in the trench where they fell, before being taken to an aid post for assessment.

Strip of lace curtain

Recycled bandages
Following the naval blockade by Britain, Germany ran out of cotton and linen. Wood fibre, paper, and lace curtains were used to make bandages.

German bandages

Forceps and clamps held securely in a metal tray

Lower tray contains saws and knives for amputation

Tools of the trade
Army doctors carried a standard set of surgical instruments. They faced a wide variety of injuries, from bullets and shell fragments.

The field hospital
Farmhouses, ruined factories, and even bombed-out churches, were used as casualty clearing stations to treat the wounded.

Shellshock

Shellshock – the collective term for concussion, emotional shock, nervous exhaustion, and similar ailments – was not identified before World War I, but trench warfare was so horrific that large numbers of soldiers developed symptoms. Most eventually recovered, but some suffered nightmares and other effects for the rest of their lives.

A medical orderly helps a wounded soldier away from the trenches

Bunks for the injured to lie on

Ambulance
The British Royal Army Medical Corps, like its German counterpart, used field ambulances to carry the wounded to hospital. Many ambulances were staffed by volunteers, often women.

Red Cross symbol to signify non-combatant status of the ambulance

Women at war

When the men went off to fight, the women had to take their place. Many women were already in work but were restricted to domestic labour, nursing, teaching, or working on the family farm – jobs considered suitable for women. Now they went to work in factories, drove trucks and ambulances, and did almost everything that only men had done before. When the war ended, most women returned to the home.

Front-line adventure
British nurse Elsie Knocker (above) went to Belgium in 1914 where she and Mairi Chisholm set up a dressing station at Pervyse. They were almost the only women on the front line, dressing the wounded until both were gassed in 1918.

Army laundry
Traditional women's work, such as working in a laundry or bakery, continued during the war on a huge scale. This British Army laundry in France cleaned the clothes of thousands of soldiers every day.

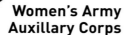

Women's Army Auxillary Corps
Many women were enlisted into auxiliary armies to release the men for the front line. They drove trucks, mended engines, and did much of the vital administration and supply work. In Britain, the recruitment poster for The Women's (later Queen Mary's) Army Auxiliary Corps described a khaki-clad woman (left) as "The girl behind the man behind the gun".

Women's Land Army

The war required a huge increase in food production at home as both sides tried to restrict the enemy's imports of food from abroad. In Britain, 113,000 women joined the Women's Land Army, set up in February 1917 to provide a well-paid female workforce to run the farms. Millions of women already worked the land across Europe.

Support your country

Images of "ideal" women were used to gain support for a country's war effort. This Russian poster urges people to buy war bonds (loans to the government).

Russia's amazons

A number of Russian women joined the "Legion of Death" to fight – and in many cases to die – for their country.

Letters to men at the front describing events at home

Family photographs

Lace handkerchief

Working in poverty

The war brought increased status and wealth to many women, but not all. In factories across Italy (above), Germany, and Russia, women worked long, hard hours but earned barely enough to feed their families. Strikes led by women were very common as a result.

Mementos from home

Women wrote letters to their husbands, brothers, and sons at the front. They often enclosed keepsakes, such as photographs or pressed flowers, to remind them of home. These did much to raise the morale of homesick and often very frightened men.

War in the air

Dogfights
Guns were mounted on top of aircraft, so pilots had to fly straight at the enemy to shoot.

When war broke out in 1914, the history of powered flight was barely ten years old. The first warplanes flew as reconnaissance craft, looking down on enemy lines or helping to direct artillery fire. Enemy pilots tried to shoot them down, leading to dogfights in the sky between highly skilled and brave "aces". Specialized fighter planes were soon produced by both sides, as were sturdier craft capable of carrying bombs.

Leather face mask

Leather balaclava

Anti-splinter glass goggles

Turned-up collar to keep neck warm

Pouch for maps

Coat of soft, supple leather

Sopwith Camel
The Sopwith F1 Camel first flew in battle in June 1917 and became the most successful Allied fighter in shooting down German aircraft.

Wooden, box-structure wings covered with canvas

Sheepskin-lined leather gloves to protect against frostbite

8.2-m (26.9-ft) wingspan

Propeller to guide the bomb

Bombs away
At first, bombs were dropped over the side of the aircraft by the pilot. Soon, specialized bomber aircraft were fitted with bombsights, bomb racks under the fuselage, and release systems.

Fins to stop the bomb from spinning on its descent

Perforated casing to help bomb catch fire on impact

Dressed for the air
Pilots flew in open cockpits, so they wore leather coats, balaclavas, and boots and gloves lined with sheepskin to keep out the cold. One-piece suits also became common.

Sheepskin boots

Thick sole to give a good grip

British 9.1-kg (20-lb) Marten Hale bomb, containing 2 kg (4.5 lb) of explosives

British Carcass incendiary bomb

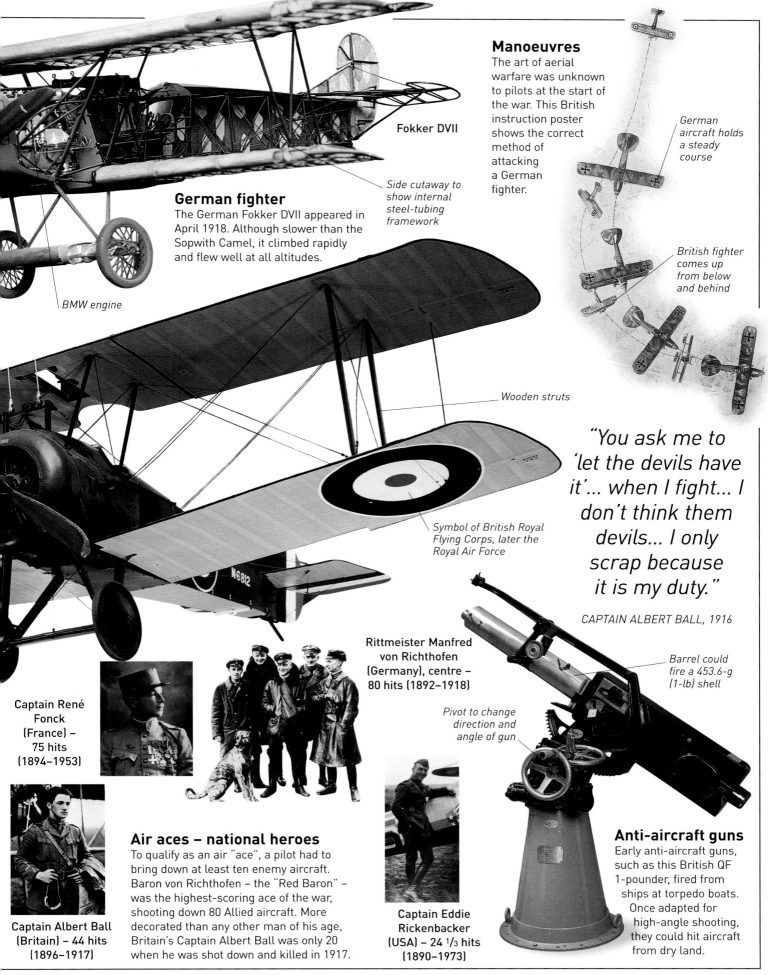

Manoeuvres

The art of aerial warfare was unknown to pilots at the start of the war. This British instruction poster shows the correct method of attacking a German fighter.

German aircraft holds a steady course

Fokker DVII

Side cutaway to show internal steel-tubing framework

German fighter

The German Fokker DVII appeared in April 1918. Although slower than the Sopwith Camel, it climbed rapidly and flew well at all altitudes.

BMW engine

British fighter comes up from below and behind

Wooden struts

"You ask me to 'let the devils have it'... when I fight... I don't think them devils... I only scrap because it is my duty."

CAPTAIN ALBERT BALL, 1916

Symbol of British Royal Flying Corps, later the Royal Air Force

Captain René Fonck (France) – 75 hits (1894–1953)

Rittmeister Manfred von Richthofen (Germany), centre – 80 hits (1892–1918)

Barrel could fire a 453.6-g (1-lb) shell

Pivot to change direction and angle of gun

Air aces – national heroes

To qualify as an air "ace", a pilot had to bring down at least ten enemy aircraft. Baron von Richthofen – the "Red Baron" – was the highest-scoring ace of the war, shooting down 80 Allied aircraft. More decorated than any other man of his age, Britain's Captain Albert Ball was only 20 when he was shot down and killed in 1917.

Captain Albert Ball (Britain) – 44 hits (1896–1917)

Captain Eddie Rickenbacker (USA) – 24 1/3 hits (1890–1973)

Anti-aircraft guns

Early anti-aircraft guns, such as this British QF 1-pounder, fired from ships at torpedo boats. Once adapted for high-angle shooting, they could hit aircraft from dry land.

Zeppelin

The first airship was designed by the German Count Ferdinand von Zeppelin in 1900. Early in the war, airships could fly higher than planes, so it was almost impossible to shoot them down. This made them useful for carrying out bombing raids. But higher flying aircraft and the use of incendiary (fire-making) bullets soon brought these aerial bombers down to earth. By 1917, most German and British airships were restricted to reconnaissance work at sea.

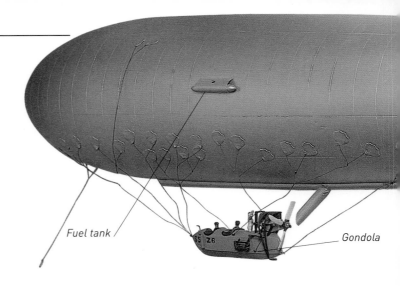

Fuel tank

Gondola

Inside the gondola
Exposed to the weather, the crew operated the airship from the open-sided gondola – a cabin below the main airship.

Bombs away!
Crews in the first airships had to drop their bombs over the side of the gondola by hand. Later models had automatic release mechanisms.

German incendiary bomb dropped by Zeppelin LZ38 on London, 31 May 1915

Getting bigger
This L3 German airship took part in the first airship raid on Britain on the night of 19–20 January 1915, causing 20 civilian casualties and enormous panic.

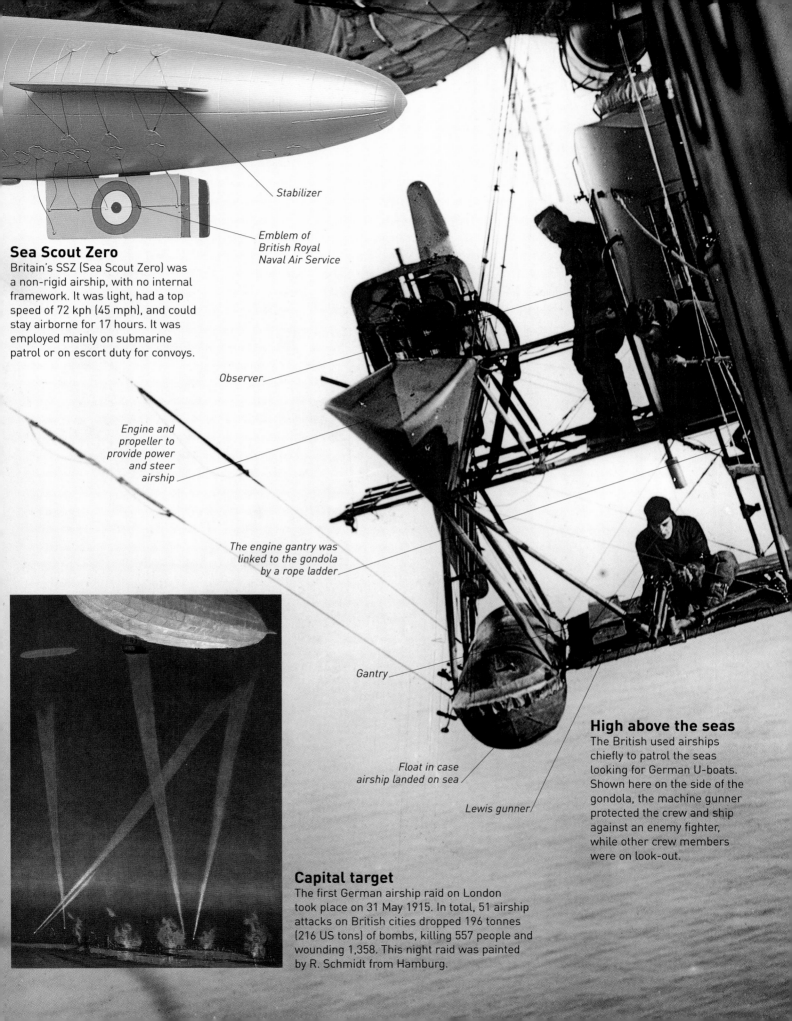

Stabilizer

Emblem of British Royal Naval Air Service

Sea Scout Zero
Britain's SSZ (Sea Scout Zero) was a non-rigid airship, with no internal framework. It was light, had a top speed of 72 kph (45 mph), and could stay airborne for 17 hours. It was employed mainly on submarine patrol or on escort duty for convoys.

Observer

Engine and propeller to provide power and steer airship

The engine gantry was linked to the gondola by a rope ladder

Gantry

Float in case airship landed on sea

Lewis gunner

High above the seas
The British used airships chiefly to patrol the seas looking for German U-boats. Shown here on the side of the gondola, the machine gunner protected the crew and ship against an enemy fighter, while other crew members were on look-out.

Capital target
The first German airship raid on London took place on 31 May 1915. In total, 51 airship attacks on British cities dropped 196 tonnes (216 US tons) of bombs, killing 557 people and wounding 1,358. This night raid was painted by R. Schmidt from Hamburg.

War at sea

The war was fought largely on land, with both sides avoiding naval conflict. The British fleet had to keep the seas open for merchant ships bringing food and other supplies to Britain, and prevent supplies reaching Germany. Germany needed its fleet to protect itself against possible invasion. The main fight took place under the sea, as German U-boats attacked Allied ships.

"I want you"
When the USA entered the war in April 1917, a recruiting poster had this attractive woman in naval uniform.

Constant threat
This German poster, *The U-boats are out!*, shows the threat posed to Allied shipping by the German U-boat fleet.

Life inside a U-boat
Conditions inside a U-boat were cramped, and fumes and heat from the engine made the air very stuffy. The crew had to navigate their craft through minefields and avoid detection in order to attack enemy ships.

Floats for landing on water

Land and sea
Seaplanes can take off and land on both water and the ground. Used for reconnaissance and bombing, they could sink an enemy ship with a torpedo.

Observation balloon

Gun

Success and failure
German U-boats operated under the sea and on the surface. Here, a deck cannon fires at an enemy steamer. The U-boats sank 5,554 Allied and neutral merchant ships as well as many warships. But 178 of the 372 U-boats were destroyed by Allied bombs or torpedoes.

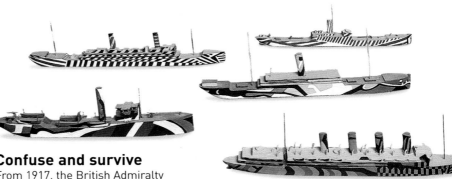

Confuse and survive

From 1917, the British Admiralty camouflaged merchant ships and their escorts with grey, black, and blue geometric patterns. This distorted the silhouette of the ship and made it difficult for German U-boats to target.

Dazzled

Many artists contributed to their country's war effort, some in surprising ways. The British painter Edward Wadsworth supervised the application of "dazzle" camouflage to ships' hulls. He later painted the picture above, *Dazzle ships in dry dock at Liverpool*, showing the finished result.

Medals awarded to Jack Cornwall

Victoria Cross (VC)

British War Medal

Victory Medal

Boy at the Battle of Jutland

John Travers Cornwall was only 16 when he first saw action at Jutland, the war's only major sea battle, on 31 May 1916. Mortally wounded, he stayed at his post until the end of the action.

The British Grand Fleet

Britain's Royal Navy was the biggest in the world and followed the "two-power standard" – its might equalled that of the two next strongest nations combined. Despite this superiority, the navy played a more limited role in the war compared with the army, keeping the seas free of German ships and escorting merchant convoys.

Flight deck

HMS *Furious*

Aircraft carriers first saw service in World War I. On 7 July 1918, seven Sopwith Camels took off from HMS *Furious* to attack a zeppelin base at Tondern in northern Germany.

Tasty greetings
A British army biscuit was so hard, a soldier in Gallipoli wrote this Christmas card on it.

Gallipoli

In 1915, the Allies tried to force through the Dardanelles Strait and take the Ottoman Turkish capital, Constantinople. Two attacks failed. On 25 April, British, Australian, and New Zealand troops landed on the Gallipoli peninsula. In August, there was a second landing on the peninsula, at Suvla Bay, but the Allies were trapped by fierce Turkish resistance. The death rate mounted, and the Allies eventually withdrew in January 1916.

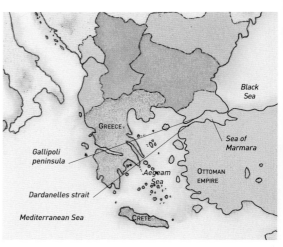

Gallipoli peninsula
The Gallipoli peninsula lies to the north of the Dardanelles. Britain and France wanted direct access from the Mediterranean to the Black Sea and their ally, Russia. But the narrow waterway was controlled by Germany's ally, the Ottoman Empire.

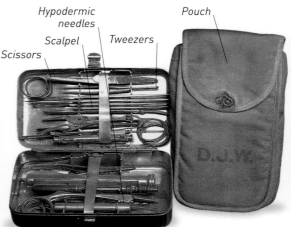

Privately purchased medical kit used by a British officer on the front line

Hypodermic needles · *Pouch* · *Scalpel* · *Tweezers* · *Scissors*

The casualty rate
The treatment and evacuation of casualties from Gallipoli was complicated by the huge numbers of sick soldiers as well as those who were wounded.

Jetty for boats carrying sick and wounded soldiers

The sick beach
On both sides, food was contaminated by flies carrying disease from the many corpses. Dysentery was rife – most of the Anzac troops in a hospital at Anzac Cove (above) had it.

German help
To the Allies' surprise, Gallipoli was strongly defended by Turkish trenches, barbed-wire fences, and artillery. Germany also equipped the Turks with modern pistols, rifles, and machine guns.

Improvised grenades
The fighting at Gallipoli was often at very close range. In a munitions shortage, Allied troops used jam tins to make hand-thrown grenades.

Narrow beach unprotected against Tukish fire

Turkish defences look down on beach

Kemal Atatürk

Mustafa Kemal was divisional commander at Gallipoli. He helped to build up the Ottoman Turkish defences and brilliantly led the 19th Division on the ridges above Anzac Cove, preventing the Allies from penetrating inland. After the war, he led a revolt to preserve Turkey. As the Turkish Republic's first president, he became known as Atatürk (Father of the Turks).

Anzac Cove

The Australian and New Zealand Army Corps, known as the Anzacs, landed on the western coast of the Gallipoli peninsula. The narrow beach and steep, sandy hills gave the men no cover. They were under constant fire from the well-hidden Ottoman Turks above.

Hyde Park Memorial, Sydney, Australia

Anzac memorial

In the war, Australia lost 60,000 men from a population of under five million. New Zealand lost 17,000 from a population of one million. Of those, 11,100 died at Gallipoli. The two countries remember their war dead on Anzac Day, 25 April.

Sultan's Cypher with the year 1333 in the Muslim calendar, which is 1915 in the Western calendar

For distinction

Created in 1915, the Turkish Order of the Crescent was awarded to German and Turkish soldiers who fought at Gallipoli.

Winter evacuation

When the Allies decided to withdraw from Gallipoli, a flotilla of ships evacuated the troops and their supplies. Unlike the chaos and carnage of the previous six months, the withdrawals under the cover of darkness went without a hitch and not one man was injured.

Many soldiers were suffering from frostbite

Large, horse-drawn gun

British soldiers evacuated by raft from Suvla Bay, 19 December 1915

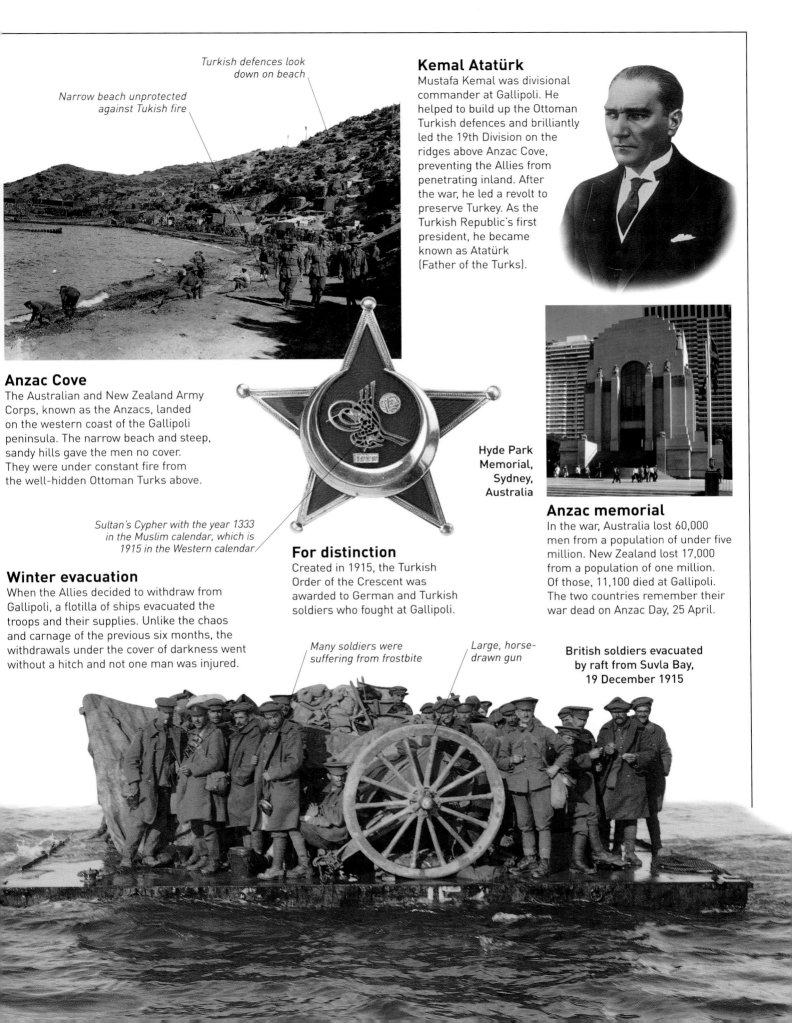

Verdun

On 21 February 1916, Germany launched a massive attack against Verdun, a fortified French city. Close to the German border, Verdun controlled access into eastern France. After a huge, eight-hour artillery bombardment, the German infantry advanced. The French were caught by surprise, but held out. By December, the Germans had been pushed back almost to where they started. The human cost was enormous – more than 400,000 French casualties and 336,831 German casualties.

Burning wreckage
On 25 February, the ancient city of Verdun was evacuated. Many buildings were hit by the artillery bombardment, and even more were destroyed by fires that often raged for days.

General Pétain
General Henri-Philippe Pétain took command of the French forces of Verdun on 25 February. He organized effective defences and army supplies. His rallying cry, "Ils ne passeront pas!" (They shall not pass!), raised French morale.

Exposed concrete fort wall

Machine-gun post

Double-breasted greatcoat

Horizon-blue uniform

Haversack

Le poilu
Nicknamed *les poilus*, or "the hairy ones", French infantry bore the brunt of the German attack. Cold, muddy, and wet, they suffered dreadful injuries from shellfire and gas.

Fort Douaumont
Verdun was protected by three rings of fortifications. Fort Douaumont, in the outer ring, was the strongest of these forts. Defended by just 56 elderly reservists, it fell to the Germans on 25 February.

Lebel rifle

Steel helmet

Thick boots with puttees wrapped around the legs

Background picture: Ruined Verdun cityscape, 1915

At close quarters

Fighting at Verdun was fierce, as both sides repeatedly attacked and counter-attacked the same forts and strategic areas around the city. Advancing attackers were mown down by machine-gun fire from inside the forts. The open ground was too exposed for rescuers to retrieve the dead, and corpses were left to rot. This photograph comes from one of many dramatic films that were made about the war.

"What a bloodbath, what horrid images, what a slaughter. I just cannot find the words to express my feelings. Hell cannot be this dreadful."

ALBERT JOUBAIRE
FRENCH SOLDIER, VERDUN, 1916

Surrounding villages

Ornes was one of many villages attacked and captured during the German advance on Verdun. This village, like eight others, was never rebuilt, but is still marked on maps as a sign of remembrance.

Laurel-leaf wreath

Oak-leaf wreath

Head of Marianne, symbol of France

Légion d'Honneur

In tribute to the people of Verdun's suffering, the French president awarded the *Légion d'Honneur* to the city. It is usually given for individual acts of bravery.

The muddy inferno

The land around Verdun is wooded and hilly, with many streams running down to the River Meuse. Heavy rainfall and constant artillery bombardment turned it into a desolate mudbath, where the dead lay half-buried in shell craters and the living had to eat and sleep within centimetres of fallen comrades. This photograph shows the "Ravine de la mort", the Ravine of the Dead.

In the east

The Western Front was locked in trench warfare, but on the other side of Europe, a much more fluid war took place. The armies of Germany and Austria-Hungary on one side and Russia on the other marched across hundreds of kilometres. The Russians and Austro-Hungarians were badly led and poorly equipped, and suffered huge losses. By 1916, the German army was in full control of the entire Eastern Front.

Tannenberg, 1914
In August 1914, Russia's First and Second armies invaded East Prussia, Germany. The Second Army was surrounded at Tannenberg and forced to surrender on 31 August, with the loss of 150,000 men and all of its artillery (above).

Masurian Lakes, 1914
In September 1914, the Russian First Army had marched to the Masurian Lakes in East Prussia and found itself in danger of being surrounded. German troops dug trenches and other defences (above) and attacked the Russians, who soon withdrew, sustaining more than 100,000 casualties. By the end of September, the Russian threat to Germany was over.

Initial success
During 1914, the Russian army took Austria-Hungary's eastern province of Galicia. In 1915, German troops (above) pushed the Russians back to Russia.

Unwilling to fight

By the end of 1916, many Russian soldiers were refusing to fight. Starving and badly treated, they saw litte reason to risk their lives in a war they did not believe in. Such low morale led, in part, to the Russian Revoution of 1917.

Russian troops marching to defend the newly captured city of Przemysl in Austrian Galicia

The Italian Front

On 23 May 1915, Italy joined the war on the side of the Allies and prepared to invade its hostile neighbour, Austria-Hungary. Fighting took place on two fronts, to Italy's north and east. The Italian army was ill-prepared and under-equipped for the war, and was unable to break through Austrian defences until its final success at the Battle of Vittorio-Veneto in October 1918.

The Isonzo River

The Isonzo flowed between the mountains of Austria-Hungary and the plains of northeast Italy. After 11 battles along the river, victory fell to the Austrians, with German support, at Caporetto in 1917.

Italian alpinists

Most of the 640-km (400-mile) Italian frontier with Austria-Hungary lay in the Italian Alps. Both sides used trained alpine troops to fight in mountainous terrain.

War in the desert

World War I was not restricted to Europe. A major conflict took place in the Middle East, which was largely controlled by the Turkish Ottoman Empire. British and Indian troops invaded Mesopotamia (now Iraq) in 1914 and took Baghdad in 1917. A large British force, under General Allenby, captured Palestine and the Syrian capital of Damascus. In Arabia, Bedouin soldiers under the guidance of T.E. Lawrence rose in revolt against Turkish rule.

Spine pad
Worried about heatstroke, the British army issued spine pads to protect soldiers' backs from the desert sun. But the heavy pads would have done little to keep the body cool.

Arab flintlock pistol

Lawrence's rifle

Lawrence's initials

Return journey
British soldier T.E. Lawrence's rifle was one of many captured by the Turks at Gallipoli in 1915. It was then given to the Arab leader, Emir Feisal, who presented it to Lawrence in 1916.

Lawrence of Arabia
T.E. Lawrence became the legendary figure known as Lawrence of Arabia. As liaison officer to Emir Feisal, leader of the Arab revolt against Ottoman Turkish rule, Lawrence helped the Arabs to become an effective guerrilla force. They blew up railway lines, attacked garrisons, and tied down an army many times their own size.

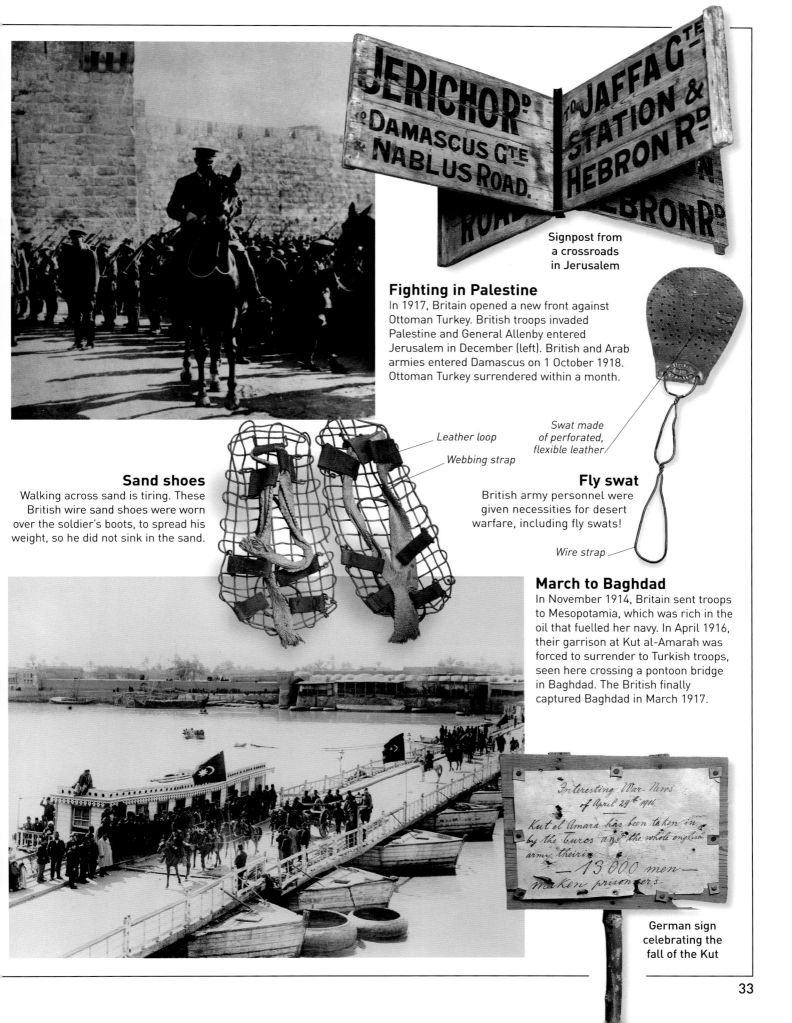

Signpost from
a crossroads
in Jerusalem

Fighting in Palestine

In 1917, Britain opened a new front against Ottoman Turkey. British troops invaded Palestine and General Allenby entered Jerusalem in December (left). British and Arab armies entered Damascus on 1 October 1918. Ottoman Turkey surrendered within a month.

Swat made
of perforated,
flexible leather

Leather loop

Webbing strap

Sand shoes

Walking across sand is tiring. These British wire sand shoes were worn over the soldier's boots, to spread his weight, so he did not sink in the sand.

Fly swat

British army personnel were given necessities for desert warfare, including fly swats!

Wire strap

March to Baghdad

In November 1914, Britain sent troops to Mesopotamia, which was rich in the oil that fuelled her navy. In April 1916, their garrison at Kut al-Amarah was forced to surrender to Turkish troops, seen here crossing a pontoon bridge in Baghdad. The British finally captured Baghdad in March 1917.

German sign
celebrating the
fall of the Kut

Espionage

Both sides suspected the other of employing hundreds of spies in enemy territory, but most espionage work consisted of eavesdropping on enemy communications. Code-breaking or cryptography was crucial, as both sides sent and received coded messages by radio and telegraph. Cryptographers devised complex codes to ensure the safe transit of their own messages while using their skills to intercept and break coded enemy messages.

Lightweight, but strong, string attaches parachute to bird

Corselet made of linen and padded to protect bird

Pigeon post

Over 500,000 pigeons were used to carry messages between intelligence agents and their home bases. The pigeons were dropped by parachute into occupied areas and collected by agents. Messages were attached to their legs, and they were released to fly back to their lofts.

In miniature

Pigeons can't carry much weight. This message is written on the small "pigeon post" form used by the German army. Long messages were photographed with a camera that reduced them to the size of a microdot – 300 times smaller than the original.

Edith Cavell

British-born Edith Cavell ran a nursing school in the Belgian city of Brussels (above). When the Germans occupied the city in August 1914, she took in up to 200 British soldiers trapped behind enemy lines. When the Germans had her shot as a spy in October 1915, her story provided powerful propaganda for the Allies.

Front of button

Coded message on back of button

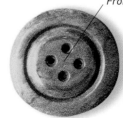

Secret ink

Special ink was used to write invisible messages on paper. The message could be read later when treated with a chemical to make the words visible.

German invisible ink   **Invisible ink bottle**

Button message

Tiny and unobtrusive, coded messages were stamped on to the back of buttons sewn on to coats or jackets.

Pocket camera

Lens cap

This miniature camera disguised as a fob watch was used to take secret photographs in German East Africa (now Tanzania).

Camera lens

Shutter release

Reading the enemy

Army intelligence officers, such as this British soldier, played a vital role in examining and understanding captured enemy documents. They pieced together information about enemy plans or morale, and sent it to the military high command.

Hidden messages

Two Dutch agents sent to England to spy for Germany pretended to be cigar importers. They used their cigar orders as codes for the ships they observed in Portsmouth Harbour. In 1915, they were caught and executed.

Cigars slit open in search of hidden messages

Aid to escape

This food tin was sent to British Lieutenant Jack Shaw at a German prisoner-of-war camp in 1918. It contained maps, wire cutters, and compasses for a mass escape.

Rolled-up map of France

Lead weights to make the tin the correct weight

Compass

Mata Hari

Dutch-born Margaretha Zelle was a famous dancer who used the stage name Mata Hari. She had many high-ranking lovers, who revealed confidential information, which she passed to the French secret service. When fed false information by a German diplomat, she was shot as a German spy in 1917.

Tank warfare

In November 1917, at the Battle of Cambrai, the British-invented tank first displayed its full potential. An artillery bombardment would have made the ground impossible for the infantry to cross. Instead, tanks flattened barbed-wire, crossed enemy trenches, and shielded the advancing infantry. Tanks played a vital role in the Allied advances throughout 1918.

Stabilizer wheels

British Mark I tank
The first tank to see action was the British Mark 1 tank. Of the 49 built for the Battle of the Somme on 15 September 1916, only 18 were judged fit for battle.

Carried crew of eight men

Total weight of 28,450 kg (62,722 lb)

Equipped with two six-pounder guns and four machine guns

Toughened leather skull cap

Protect and survive
British tank crews wore leather helmets with visors and chainmail mouthpieces to protect their heads against specks of hot metal that flew off the inside of the hull when the tank was hit by bullets.

Leather visor

Chainmail mouthpiece

German A7V tank

British Mark V tank

A7V tank
In 1918, too late to make any real impact, the Germans built the huge A7V, a 33,500-kg (73,855-lb) machine with six machine guns and a crew of 18. Only 20 A7Vs were constructed.

Inside a tank
The tank was hot, fume-ridden, and badly ventilated, making the crew sick or even faint. The heat was sometimes so great in light tanks that it exploded the ammunition.

Rear entry hatch

Driver's entry hatch

Lid for driver's entry hatch

Driver's visor

T 9171

ME 9828

Iron caterpillar track

The driver and gunner were squashed in the front of the tank

Six men sat around the engine manning the guns

Six-cylinder engine

British Mark V tank
The British Mark V tank first saw action in July 1918. It had two six-pounder guns and four machine guns, and had a crew of eight.

Machine-gun port

Driving a tank
Early tanks were driven by two people, each controlling one track, and had a range of just 40 km (25 miles). Later tanks had a single driver, but they were still vulnerable to enemy shellfire, and often broke down, as here during the British assault on Arras in 1917.

Crossing the trenches
For wide trenches, British tanks were fitted with circular metal bundles that dropped into the trench to form a bridge. This line of Mark V tanks is moving in to attack German trenches in autumn 1918.

The USA joins in

When war broke out in Europe in 1914, the USA remained neutral. In 1917, Germany decided to attack all foreign shipping to try to limit supplies to Britain. It also tried to divert US attention from Europe by encouraging its neighbour, Mexico, to invade. This action outraged the US government, and as more US ships were sunk, President Wilson declared war on Germany. This was now a world war.

Uncle Sam
The all-American figure of Uncle Sam was based on Kitchener's pose for British recruiting posters (see p. 14). Beneath his pointing finger were the words "I WANT YOU FOR THE US ARMY".

British medal suggesting the attack on SS *Lusitania* was planned

SS Lusitania
On 7 May 1915, the passenger ship SS *Lusitania* was sunk off the Irish coast by German torpedoes, for allegedly carrying munitions. The victims included 128 US citizens. Their death did much to turn the US public against Germany and towards the Allies.

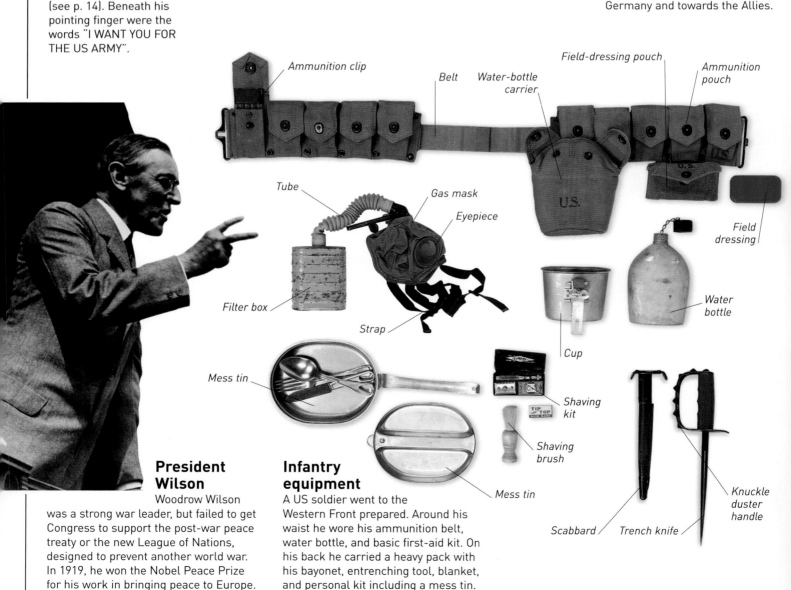

Ammunition clip · Belt · Water-bottle carrier · Field-dressing pouch · Ammunition pouch

Tube · Gas mask · Eyepiece

Filter box · Strap

Field dressing · Water bottle

Cup

Mess tin · Shaving kit · Shaving brush · Mess tin

Scabbard · Trench knife · Knuckle duster handle

President Wilson
Woodrow Wilson was a strong war leader, but failed to get Congress to support the post-war peace treaty or the new League of Nations, designed to prevent another world war. In 1919, he won the Nobel Peace Prize for his work in bringing peace to Europe.

Infantry equipment
A US soldier went to the Western Front prepared. Around his waist he wore his ammunition belt, water bottle, and basic first-aid kit. On his back he carried a heavy pack with his bayonet, entrenching tool, blanket, and personal kit including a mess tin.

Gun fire
The US First Army first saw major action in September 1918 at St Mihiel, south of Verdun, France, in an Allied attack on German lines. Here an artillery crew fires a field gun, surrounded by shell cases.

For heroism
Introduced in 1918, the Distinguished Service Cross was awarded for extreme heroism against an armed enemy.

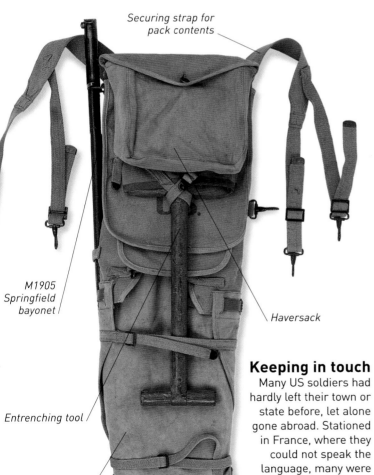

Securing strap for pack contents

M1905 Springfield bayonet

Haversack

Entrenching tool

Blanket or greatcoat roll

Assembled kit, US infantry equipment

Keeping in touch
Many US soldiers had hardly left their town or state before, let alone gone abroad. Stationed in France, where they could not speak the language, many were homesick. They wrote often to family and friends, and waited for letters, postcards, and food parcels in return.

Mines and mud

Air tubes

To the rescue
Fumes from a gas attack or a shell burst near a tunnel entrance could suffocate the men inside. This German breathing apparatus was for rescue parties.

For much of the war on the Western Front, the two sides faced each other in rows of heavily fortified trenches. Both excavated tunnels and mines deep under enemy lines and packed them with explosives, ready to be detonated when an attack began. Counter-mines were dug to destroy enemy mines before they could be finished. Vast mines were exploded by the British at the Battle of the Somme on 1 July 1916, but their most effective use was at the start of the Battle of Passchendaele.

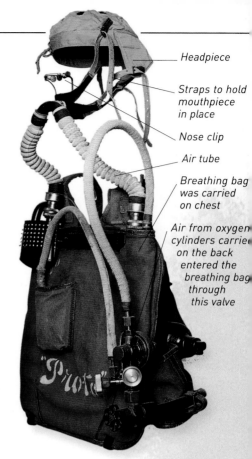

Headpiece

Straps to hold mouthpiece in place

Nose clip

Air tube

Breathing bag was carried on chest

Air from oxygen cylinders carried on the back entered the breathing bag through this valve

Oxygen relief
This British breathing apparatus, like the German equipment on the left, fed compressed oxygen to a mouthpiece to help a miner breathe.

Background picture: a British mine explodes under German lines at the Battle of the Somme, 1 July 1916

Sappers at work
British artist David Bomberg painted members of the Royal Engineers, known as sappers, digging and reinforcing this underground trench.

"It is horrible. You often wish you were dead, there is no shelter, we are lying in water... our clothes do not dry."

GERMAN SOLDIER, PASSCHENDAELE, 1917

Waterlogged
The water table around Ypres was very high, so the trenches were built above ground by banking up earth and sandbags. Even so, the trenches were constantly flooded. Pumping out mines and trenches, as these Australian tunnellers are doing at Hooge, Belgium, in September 1917, was an essential, never-ending task.

Passchendaele

In 1917, the British planned to attack the German front line around Ypres, Belgium, and then seize the channel ports used by German submarines as a base to attack British shipping. The Battle of Messines began on 7 June 1917. After a huge artillery bombardment, 19 mines packed with one million tonnes (1.1 million US tons) of explosives blew up under the German lines on Messines Ridge. The noise could be heard in London 220 km (140 miles) away. The village and ridge of Passchendaele were captured on 10 November 1917, then lost again. In summer 1918, the Allies re-captured and kept the ground.

Muddy quagmire
Heavy rainfall and constant shelling at Passchendaele created a deadly mudbath. Many injured men died as they were unable to lift themselves clear of the cloying mud. Stretcher bearers were barely able to carry the wounded to dressing stations.

British troops moving forward over shell-torn ground during the Battle of Passchendaele

The final year

In early 1918, the war looked to be turning in favour of Germany. Russia had withdrawn from the war, so Germany could now focus on the Western Front, and most US troops had yet to reach France. But the Allied blockade of her ports kept Germany short of vital supplies, food was scarce, and strikes and mutinies were rife. Ottoman Turkey, Bulgaria, and Austria-Hungary collapsed under Allied attack. By early November, Germany stood alone. On 7 November, a German delegation crossed the front line to discuss peace terms with the Allies.

New leader
In 1917, Vladimir Lenin, the anti-war leader of the Bolshevik (Communist) Party, became the new ruler of Russia.

Germans and Russians celebrate the cease-fire on the Eastern Front, 1917

Russia pulls out

The Russian government became increasingly unpopular as the war progressed. In February 1917, a revolution overthrew the Tsar, but the new government continued the war. A second revolution in October brought the Bolshevik Party to power. A ceasefire was agreed with Germany, and in March 1918 Russia signed the Treaty of Brest-Litovsk and withdrew from the war.

The Ludendorff Offensive
General Ludendorff launched a huge attack on the Western Front on 21 March 1918, hoping to defeat Britain and France before US troops arrived. Germany advanced almost 64 km (40 miles) by July, but suffered 500,000 casualties.

French and British troops in action during the Ludendorff Offensive

3 March Treaty of Brest-Litovsk; Russia leaves the war
21 March Vast Ludendorff Offensive on the Western Front

15 July Last German offensive launched on Western Front
18 July French counter-attack begins on the Marne

8 August British launch offensive near Amiens
12 September Americans launch offensive at St Mihiel

14 September Allies attack Bulgaria from Greece
25 September Bulgaria seeks peace

Battle of the Marne

On 18 July 1918, French and US forces counter-attacked against the German advance on the River Marne, east of Paris, and began to push the Germans eastwards. By 6 August, the Germans had lost 168,000 men, many buried where they fell on the battlefields (left). The Allies now had the upper hand.

French soldiers identifying German dead before burial

Crossing the line

On 8 August 1918, a huge British offensive began near Amiens. Allied troops were pushing towards the heavily fortified Hindenburg Line, the Germans' fall-back defensive position. On 29 September, the British 46th North Midland Division took the bridge at Riqueval. They had broken the Line at last, and posed for this photograph.

Many French children did not remember life before the German occupation of their towns and cities

Background picture: German troops advancing at the Somme, April 1918

French children march alongside the Allied army

The last days

By 5 October, the Allies had breached the entire Hindenburg Line. Both sides suffered great casualties as the German army was pushed steadily eastwards. As the British and French recaptured towns and cities lost in 1914, including Lille (left), the German retreat was turning into a defeat.

27 September British begin to breach Hindenburg Line
1 October British take Ottoman Turkish-held Damascus

6 October German government starts to negotiate an armistice
24 October Italy attacks Austria-Hungary at Vittorio-Veneto

29 October German fleet mutinies
30 October Ottoman Turkey agrees an armistice
4 November Austria-Hungary

agrees an armistice
9 November The Kaiser abdicates
11 November Armistice between Germany and the Allies; war ends

Armistice and peace

Carriage talks
On 7 November 1918, a German delegation met the Allied commander-in-chief, Marshal Foch, in his railway carriage in the forest of Compiègne. On 11 November, they signed an armistice agreement.

At 11 am on the 11th day of the 11th month of 1918, the guns of Europe fell silent after more than four years of war. The Allies wanted to make sure that Germany would never go to war again. The eventual peace treaty redrew the map of Europe and forced Germany to pay huge damages to the Allies. German armed forces were reduced and Germany lost a great deal of land and all of her overseas colonies.

Displaced people
Many refugees, like these Lithuanians, were displaced during the war. The end of hostilities allowed thousands of refugees to return to their newly liberated countries. There were also as many as 6.5 million prisoners of war who had to be repatriated. This complex task was finally achieved by autumn 1919.

Spreading the news
News of the armistice spread around the world in minutes, in newspapers and telegrams, and by word of mouth in every neighbourhood.

Vive la paix!
In Paris (below), Allied soldiers joined locals in an inpromptu procession. In London, women and children danced in the streets while their men prepared to leave the front. In Germany, there was shock and relief that the fighting was over.

Signing the treaty
These soldiers watching the signing of the Treaty of Versailles had waited a long time for this moment. The Allies first met their German counterparts in January 1919. Negotiations almost broke down several times before a final agreement was reached in June 1919.

The Treaty of Versailles
The peace treaty that ended the war was signed in the Hall of Mirrors in the Palace of Versailles near Paris, on 28 June 1919. William Orpen's painting shows the four Allied leaders watching the German delegates sign the treaty.

The peace treaties
The Treaty of Versailles was signed by representatives of the Allied powers and Germany. Over the next year, in the Allies' treaties with Austria, Bulgaria, Turkey, and Hungary, a new map of Europe emerged.

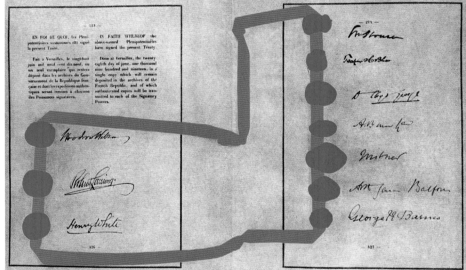

The Treaty of Versailles

General Foch

Georges Clemenceau

David Lloyd George

Vittorio Orlando

Giorgio Sonnino

The victorious allies
The negotiations in Paris were dominated by the Big Four: French premier Georges Clemenceau (supported by General Foch), British premier David Lloyd George, Italian premier Vittorio Orlando (seen here with his foreign minister, Giorgio Sonnino), and the US president Woodrow Wilson.

The cost of war

One life
A soldier remembers a fallen comrade during the Battle of Passchendaele in 1917, but many men were engulfed in mud, their graves unmarked.

The human cost of this war was huge. Over 65 million men fought, of whom more than half were killed or injured – eight million killed, two million died of illness and disease, 21.2 million wounded, and 7.8 million taken prisoner or missing. About 6.6 million civilians also perished. Among the combatant nations, apart from the USA, there was barely a family that had not lost at least one son or brother. European economies were ruined, while the USA emerged as a major world power.

The unknown soldier
Many of the dead were too badly disfigured to be identified. Thousands more just disappeared, presumed dead. Tombs of an unknown warrior stand at the Arc de Triomphe, Paris, and Westminster Abbey, London.

Aftercare
For thousands of disfigured and disabled soldiers, reconstructive surgery helped repair facial damage, masks and prosthetics covered horrible disfigurements, and artificial limbs gave some mobility.

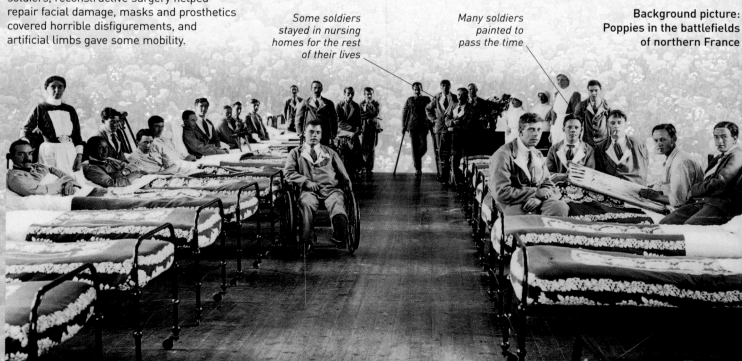

Some soldiers stayed in nursing homes for the rest of their lives

Many soldiers painted to pass the time

Background picture: Poppies in the battlefields of northern France

Mementos

Soldiers on both sides of the Western Front pressed wild flowers as mementos. Private Jack Mudd sent this red Flanders poppy to his wife Lizzie before he was killed at Passchendaele. The poppies feature in the wartime poem *In Flanders Fields*, and inspired the British Legion to sell paper poppies to raise money for injured soldiers and as a sign of remembrance for the dead.

War memorials

The Western Front is lined with graveyards and memorials to the fallen, including 130,000 unknown French and German soldiers at Douaumont, Verdun (below).

Prussian Iron Cross

Victoria Cross (V.C.)

For gallantry

Every combatant nation awarded medals for bravery to its soldiers, civilians, and allies – including five million Iron Crosses in Germany, over two million Croix de Guerre in France, and 576 Victoria Crosses across the British Empire.

French *Croix de Guerre*

Index

A
aerial:
  reconnaissance 22
  warfare 21
air aces 21
aircraft 20–21
aircraft carriers 25
airships 22–23
Allenby, General 32, 33
Allies 7, 15, 26
  and peace 44, 45
  see also individual countries
ambulances, field 17
Annamites 6
anti-aircraft guns 21
Anzac:
  Cove 26, 27
  Day 27
armistice 43, 44
army doctors and
  medical officers
  15, 17
artillery 12–13, 28, 41
Asquith, Herbert 8
Atatürk, Kemal 27
Australia 6, 26, 27
Austria-Hungary 2, 3,
  30, 42
auxiliary armies 18

BC
Ball, Albert 21
Belgium 2, 3, 4, 5, 7, 41
Berryman, Captain 5
Big Four 45
bombardment 12–13, 14, 28
Bomberg, David 40
bombing raids 22, 23
bombs 20, 22
Bosnia 2
breathing apparatus 40
Brest-Litovsk, Treaty of 42
Britain 2, 3, 7
  army 6, 7, 8, 9
British Expeditionary Force
  (B.E.F.) 4
British Legion 47
Bulgaria 42
Cambrai, Battle of 36
cameras, spy 34, 35
camouflage 25
Canada 6
Caporetto 31
carrier pigeons 34

casualties 16–17, 26, 28, 30,
  42, 46
Cavell, Edith 34
Chisholm, Mairi 18
Christmas 4, 5, 26
Clemenceau, Georges 45
codes 34
conscientious objectors 9
conscription 8
constant barrage 12
Cornwall, John Travers
  25
counter-mines 40
Croix de Guerre 47
cryptography 34

DEF
Dardanelles Strait 26
desert war 32–33
Distinguished Service
  Cross 39
dogfights 20
Douaumont, Fort 28
dressing station 18
Eastern Europe 6
Eastern Front 30
  ceasefire 42
enlisting 8
espionage 34–35
Feisal, Emir 32
fighter planes 20, 21
Fokker DVII 21
Sopwith F1 Camel 20
fleets:
  British 24, 25
  German 24
Foch, General 44, 45
Fonck, René 21
food 9, 19, 24, 26, 35,
  39, 42
forts 28, 29
France 2, 3
  army 3, 7
Franz, Ferdinand
  Archduke 2
fraternization 42
front line 10
HMS Furious 25

GHI
Galicia 30
Gallipoli 26–27
Germany
  army 2, 5, 7
  declarations of war 2, 3
  and peace 44, 45
  graves 46, 47
Greece 6
grenades 7, 26

gunners 13, 23
guns:
  howitzer 12, 13
  machine guns, British
  and German 14
  Mark I 4
helmets 7, 12, 36
Hindenburg
  Line 43
hospitals 16, 17, 26
In Flanders Fields 47
intelligence gathering
  34, 35
invisible ink 34
Iron Cross 47
iron ration 9
Isonzo River 31
Italian Front 31
Italy 3, 31, 43

JKL
Japan 6, 7
Jutland, Battle of 25
Kitchener, Lord 8
Knocker, Elsie 18
Lawrence, T.E.
  (Lawrence of Arabia)
  32
Légion d'Honneur 29
Lenin, Vladimir 42
letters 19, 39
Lloyd George, David 45
Ludendorff Offensive 42
SS Lusitania 38
Luxembourg 3

MNO
machine guns 4, 14, 15
Marne, Battle of the 4, 43
Masurian Lakes 30
Mata Hari 35
medals 25, 27, 29,
  39, 47
medical:
  aid 16, 17
  officers 15
Mesopotamia 32, 33
Messines Ridge 41
microdots 34
mines 40, 41
mobilization 2, 3
Montenegro 6, 7
Mudd, Private Jack 47
Néry, Battle of 4
New Zealand 6, 26, 27
Nicholas, Grand Duke 6
Nicholas II, Tsar 6, 42
no-man's-land 5, 14
Orlando, Vittorio 45

Ornes, France 29
Ottoman Turkey 3, 26, 27, 32, 33,
  42, 43

PRS
Palestine 32, 33
Passchendaele, Battle of 40,
  41, 46
peace terms and treaty 42, 44, 45
Pétain, General 28
pigeon post 34
pilots 20
poilu, le 7, 28
poppies 46, 47
Princip, Gavrilo 2
prisoners of war 44
rations 9
reconnaissance work 20, 22
refugees 44
remembrance 27, 29, 47
reserve:
  armies 2, 6, 7
  Richthofen, Baron von (Red
  Baron) 21
rifles
  Lawrence's, T.E. 32
  Lebel 7, 28
  Lee Enfield 6
  Mauser 7
Riqueval, bridge at 43
Royal Engineers 40
Russia 2, 3, 4
  Eastern Front 30
  revolution 31, 42
  soldiers 6, 31
  withdrawal from war 42
sappers 40
Sarajevo, Bosnia 2
Schlieffen plan 4
sea battle 24, 25
seaplanes 24
Serbia 2, 6
shells 12, 13
  classification of 13
shellshock 17
shrapnel 13
Somme, Battle of the 15, 36, 40
South Africa 6
spies 34–35
SSZ (Sea Scout Zero) airship 23
surgical kits, portable 26

TUV
tanks 13, 36–37
  British Mark I 36
  British Mark V 36, 37
  crews 36, 37
  German A7V 36
Tannenberg 30

trenches 10–11, 14–15
  duckboards 11
  fire bays 11
  over the top 14–15
  signposts 10
  tanks crossing 37
  undermining 40, 41
Turkey, see Ottoman
  Turkey
U-boats 23, 24, 25
Uncle Sam 38
uniforms 6, 7, 8, 9, 20
  basic kits 9, 38
  sand shoes 33
  spine pads 32
unknown soldier 46
USA 38–39, 42, 43, 46
Verdun 28–29, 47
Versailles, Treaty of 45
Victoria Cross 25, 47
Vittorio-Veneto, Battle
  of 31

WYZ
Wadsworth, Edward 25
war:
  artists 25, 40
  bonds 19
  loans 9
  memorials 47
  warplanes 20, 21
  weapons 10, 32
Western Europe 7
Western Front 4–5, 42, 47
  ceasefire (Armistice) 44
  front line 10
white feathers 9
Wilson, President Woodrow
  38, 45
women at war 17, 18–19
Women of Pervyse 18
Women's Army Auxiliary Corps
  (W.A.A.C.) 18
Women's Land Army 19
wounded 16–17
  rescuing of 41
  treating 15, 17, 18
Ypres, Belgium 41
zeppelins 22–23, 25

Acknowledgements

Dorling Kindersley would like to thank:
Elizabeth Bowers, Christopher Dowling, Mark Pindelski, & the photography archive team at the Imperial War Museum for their invaluable help; Right Section, Kings Own Royal Horse Artillery for firing the gun shown on page 4; Lynn Bresler for the index; the author for assisting with revisions; Claire Bowers, David Ball, Neville Graham, Rose Horridge, Joanne Little, and Susan Nicholson for the wallchart; BCP, Marianne Petrou, and Owen Peyton Jones for checking the digitized files.

For this relaunch edition, the publishers would also like to thank: Camilla Hallinan for text editing and Carron Brown for proofreading.

The publishers would also like to thank the following for their kind permission to reproduce their photographs:
a=above, b=below, c=centre, l=left, r=right, t=top

AKG London: 45, 22br, 23bl, 24cl, 24bl, 27 tr, 28c, 28bl, 29br, 24cl, 24bl, 27tr, 28c, 28bl, 29br, 36cl, 42–43t, 44c. **Corbis:** 17tr; Bettmann 2tr, 12–13, 33bl, 39tr, 21bc, 33tl, 38bl, 39t, 39br, 42–43, 45cr; Dave G. Houser 27cr. **DK Picture Library:** Andrew L. Chernack, Springfield, Pennsylvania: 39tr; Imperial War Museum 7cl,13bc, 14cl, 27c, 34bc, 35c; RAF Museum, Hendon: 20cla, 20cl; Spink and Son Ltd: 29bc. **Robert Harding Picture Library:** 47c. Heeresgeschichtliches Museum, Wien: 2bl. **Hulton Getty:** 8tl, 11tl, 19tr, 18–19b, 21clb, 22cra, 27c, 29t, 31cra, 34clb, 35cl, 42tl, 44tl, 44b, 45tr, 45b; Topical Press Agency 34cl. **Imperial War Museum:** 2tl (HU68062), 3bl (Q81763), lltr (Q70075), 4–llt (Q70232), 6clb (32002), 8bc (Q42033), 9tr (Cat. No. 0544), 9cr (Q823), 10c (Q57228), 10b (Q193), 11br (E(AUS)577), 12bl (Q104), 13tl (E921), 12–13b (Q3214), 14cr, 15tr (Q1561), 15br (Q739), 14–15b (Q53), 16tr (Q1778),16cl (Q2628), 17br (Q4502), 321, 18c (Q8537), 19tl (Q30678), 19tr (1646), 19cr (Q19134), 21cb (Q42284), 21bl (Q69593), 20–21c, 22clb, 23 (Q27488), 24tl, 24tr (PST0515), 25cr (Q20883), 25br (Q63698),

26cl (Q13618), 26br (Q13281), 27tl (Q13603), 27b (Q13637), 32cr (Q60212), 32bl, 35tr (Q26945), 36bl (Q9364), 37cr (Q6434), 37br (Q9364), 38tl (2747), Sappers at Work by David Bomberg 40cl (2708), 41tr (E(AUS)1396), 41cr (Q5935), 40–41c (Q754), 40–41b (Q2708), 42b (Q10810), 43tr (Q9534), 43b (Q9586), The Signing of Peace in the Hall of Mirrors, Versailles by Sir William Orpen 45tl (2856), 46tl (Q2756), 46c Q1540); **David King Collection:** 30bl, 31tl, 42cla. **National Gallery Of Canada, Ottawa:** Transfer from the Canadian War Memorials, Dazzle ships in dry dock at Liverpool, 1921 by Edward Wadsworth 25tl. **Peter Newark's Military Pictures:** 7ac, 28tr. **Pa Photos:** Roger-Viollet: 3tr, 3cr, llbr, 7cr; Boyer 11bl. **Telegraph Colour Library:** J.P. Fruchet 46c. **Topham Picturepoint:**28tl, 30tl, 31br, 30–31b, 46b; ASAP 29cl. **Ullstein Bild:** 2–3c, 30tl.

All other images © Dorling Kindersley.
For further information see:
www.dkimages.com